THE
COMPUTER
ALPHABET BOOK

Other Avon Camelot Books by
Elizabeth S. Wall with Alexander C. Wall

THE BEGINNER'S COMPUTER DICTIONARY

ELIZABETH S. WALL grew up in New York City and teaches computer programming to 5th graders. She now lives in Florida with her husband Alexander.

JARED LEE is an illustrator and lives in Ohio. His work has appeared in several childrens books and magazines.

THE COMPUTER ALPHABET BOOK

ELIZABETH S. WALL

ILLUSTRATED BY JARED LEE

AN AVON ◖CAMELOT BOOK

THE COMPUTER ALPHABET BOOK is an original publication of Avon Books. This work has never before appeared in book form.

2nd grade reading level has been determined using the Fry Readability Scale.

AVON BOOKS
A division of
The Hearst Corporation
1790 Broadway
New York, New York 10019

Library of Congress Cataloging in Publication Data

Wall, Elizabeth S. (Elizabeth Spooner)
  The computer alphabet book.

  Summary: A dictionary of computer-related words, from address and Basic to you and zero.
    1. Computers—Dictionaries—Juvenile literature.
[1. Computers—Dictionaries] I. Wall, Alexander C. (Alexander Casemann) II. Title.
QA76.15.W285 1984   001.64'03'21   84-45079
ISBN 0-380-87106-8

First Camelot Printing, June, 1984

Many thanks to Cheryl Bowman, Media Specialist and
Harry W. Soward, Principal, of Garden School, Venice, Florida
for their interest in the COMPUTER ALPHABET BOOK.

To Sandy and Peter
Who know all about computers
from A to Z

About the
COMPUTER ALPHABET BOOK

The COMPUTER ALPHABET BOOK is a young child's entry into the world of computers. It uses the familiar alphabet to introduce simple definitions of computer parts and terms. Some words are familiar to the reader, some are not, but all relate to the world of computers and how they work.

Identifying letters of the alphabet with computer terms is a first step to computer awareness and literacy for the elementary school child. The book is useful in the home or school for reference or independent reading.

The COMPUTER ALPHABET BOOK is a readiness book. After the book is read, the computer novice has a basic working knowledge of a small list of critical words. The easy-to-read text is accompanied by colorful illustrations that provide visual cues to stimulate the child's interest and imagination in computers.

The reader learns that a computer:

- has a memory and can read and write to it. (see memory, data, input, output, address, tape, floppy disk, program, software, write)
- has a language (see X, zero, number, END, GOTO, RUN, language, Basic)
- has parts (see keyboard, video screen, hardware, jack, computer, tape)
- needs people to make it work (see you)
- works for the user (see program, data, output)

The reader also learns...

- specific uses of a computer in school (see output, software)
- to identify the fact that there are other programming languages (see Basic, language)
- that computers are useful for tasks that require speed, accuracy, and repetitiveness (see computer)

The COMPUTER ALPHABET BOOK develops a positive attitude about computers. Readers don't need a computer to enjoy this book. They discover that the computer is friendly and, given an opportunity, will want to spend "hands-on" time using a computer at home or in school.

THE
COMPUTER
ALPHABET BOOK

A

ADDRESS The name of a place in a computer where a number or letter is stored.

Numbers and letters are stored at an address in a part of the computer called "memory." Each place in a computer's memory has an address number just like your house has an address number. There are many addresses in the computer. It can store thousands of letters and numbers.

B

BASIC The name of one computer language.

We talk to each other in the English language. To talk to computers, we need a special language like BASIC. Most home and school computers know BASIC. It's a language which uses words you can understand like **END, GOTO,** and **RUN.** You'll learn about these words as we go through the book.

C

COMPUTER A machine that can do arithmetic faster than anybody.

A computer can also read, write, count, and remember things faster and better than you or I. It never gets tired. It can work all day and all night. It never needs to stop for lunch.

D

DATA All the words and numbers the computer needs to do a job.

Data can be facts about you such as your name, address, and telephone number. Data can be facts about the things around you. Football scores, how much rain falls, or the number of books in your school library are all data. Can you think of other data?

E

END A word in BASIC that tells the computer to stop.

The word **END** tells the computer the job is all done.

FLOPPY DISK The name for a soft, round record inside a cover.

The disk is the computer's record. It's a place where data and messages for the computer are stored. Like a record, the computer can play it again and again. The cover keeps it clean. It never comes off. The disk is played with the cover on.

G

GOTO A word in BASIC telling the computer to move to a special line number.

GOTO always has a line number after it. When the computer sees **GOTO,** it moves to that numbered line. You can see that **GOTO** is two English words made into one BASIC word.

H

HARDWARE The name for all parts of the computer machine.

You can see and touch hardware. Other parts that help the computer do its work are the keyboard, video screen, tape recorder, and printer. These are all computer hardware.

I

INPUT Data and messages sent into a computer.

Your input tells the computer what to do. You can use a keyboard to type input into the computer. Another way to send input to a computer is from a cassette tape or a floppy disk.

J

JACK The place where a plug goes.
Jacks and plugs connect all parts of the
computer together with wires.

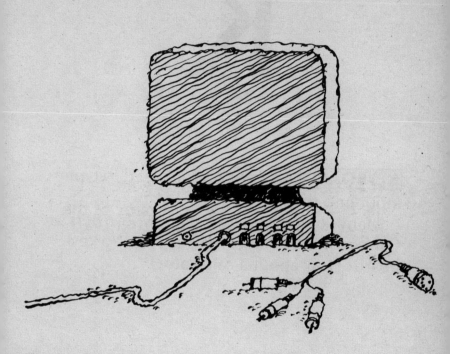

K

KEYBOARD Rows of buttons used to type input into the computer.

Many keyboards look like typewriters. Can you think of other machines with a keyboard? How about a calculator?

L

LANGUAGE Words, signs, and numbers the computer can understand.

Just like you, computers have languages. BASIC is the name of one computer language. Fortran, Cobol, Pilot, and Pascal are some other languages used in computers. You know English. Do you understand any other language?

M

MEMORY The parts of a computer where messages and data are stored.

The computer has different kinds of memory. They have names like ROM, RAM, and PROM. The floppy disk and tape cassette are also memory parts. It's like your school library, where data is stored in books, on tape, on records, or in the card catalog.

NUMBERS 0 (Zero) and 1 are what the computer uses to change all input to an inside code.

You can use words and numbers to send a message into the computer. But inside, the computer must change them to a code of zeros and ones before it can go to work, This code is a language called "machine language" and looks like this. You can see that only a machine could understand that!

OUTPUT Data and messages sent out by a computer.

Output means the message sent out of the computer to you. Output is the opposite of input. You can see output from the computer on a screen or it may be printed on paper. If you ask the computer for the names of all the children on your school bus, the list of names sent out to you is called output.

P

PROGRAM The list of orders given to a computer to tell it what to do.

A program is the message you input to the computer. Each line in a BASIC program starts with a number. Each line has a BASIC word. This program tells the computer to print a name. Try it with your name.

QUESTION MARK The sign that some computer languages use to ask you for input.

When you see "**?**" on the video screen, the computer is waiting for you to type input.

R

RUN A word in BASIC that tells the computer to go to work.

When you have finished inputting a program, type **RUN.** This tells the computer to go to work and do what you told it to do in the program.

S

SOFTWARE The name for all programs used by the computer.

Games, math drills, and other programs are all called computer software. You can buy software on a tape or disk in a computer store or make up your own programs.

T

TAPE The name for the thin plastic ribbon inside a cassette which stores computer programs and data.

Tape is one kind of memory where programs are stored. The computer listens to a program on tape just as you do. The computer can play the tape again and again. You can listen to a computer program on a tape recorder to hear the strange computer language of 0's and 1's.

U

UNIVAC The name of the first electronic computer sold.

It was very big—too big to fit into your bedroom. Today we have smaller computers called minicomputers and even smaller ones to fit on your desk called microcomputers.

VIDEO SCREEN One place where a computer sends output.

It looks like a TV screen. Some microcomputers do use a TV. Other microcomputers use a special video screen called a monitor.

WRITE A computer word that means "put data in memory."

When you write, you put words and numbers on paper. When the computer **WRITE**s, it stores words and numbers on its disk, tape, or inside memory. You can write a program on paper and then input it to the computer with the keyboard.

X

X Stands for a number or letter.

X can be used in place of any letter or number in a computer program just as you use X in a math number sentence.

Y

YOU The only way to make the computer work.

You must turn on the computer. It can't work alone. When you turn it on and tell it what to do, you and the computer will have a wonderful adventure together.

ZERO A very important part of the computer's language.

Zero is not nothing! It's part of the computer's machine language. Zero and 1 are all the computer uses to make its own machine-language code for our numbers and alphabet.

NOW YOU KNOW . . .

ADDRESS . . . the name of a place in a computer where a number or letter is stored

BASIC . . . the name of one computer language

COMPUTER . . . a machine that can do arithmetic faster than anybody

DATA . . . all the words and numbers the computer needs to do a job

END . . . a word in BASIC that tells the computer to stop

FLOPPY DISK . . . the name for a soft round record inside a cover

GOTO . . . a word in BASIC telling the computer to move to a special line number

HARDWARE . . . the name for all parts of the computer machine

INPUT . . . data and messages sent into a computer

JACK . . . the place where a plug goes

KEYBOARD . . . rows of buttons you press to type input into the computer

LANGUAGE . . . words, signs, and numbers the computer can understand

MEMORY . . . the parts of a computer where messages and data are stored

NUMBERS . . . 0 and 1 are what the computer uses to change all input to an inside code

OUTPUT . . . data and messages sent out by a computer

PROGRAM . . . list of orders given to a computer to tell it what to do

QUESTION MARK . . . the sign that some computer languages use to ask you for input

RUN . . . a word in BASIC that tells the computer to go to work

SOFTWARE . . . the name for all programs used by the computer

TAPE . . . the name for the thin plastic ribbon inside a cassette, which stores computer programs and data

UNIVAC . . . the name of the first electronic computer sold

VIDEO SCREEN . . . one place where a computer sends output

WRITE . . . a computer word that means "put data in memory"

X . . . stands for a number or letter

YOU . . . the only way to make the computer work

ZERO . . . a very important part of the computer's language

   Maybe you learned some other words about computers!